The Challenge of
WORLD
HUNGER

WILLIAM SPENCER

✦ *Environmental Issues Series* ✦

ENSLOW PUBLISHERS, INC.

Bloy St. & Ramsey Ave.
Box 777
Hillside, N.J. 07205
U.S.A.

P. O. Box 38
Aldershot
Hants GU12 6BP
U.K.

To Elizabeth, who cared and wanted the story to be told.

The author wishes to acknowledge the following for their assistance in preparing this book: Dr. John Gerber, Biotechnology Center, University of Florida; Dr. Max Langham, Institute for Food and Agricultural Sciences, University of Florida; and Alachua County science teachers.

Library of Congress Cataloging-in-Publication Data
Spencer, William, 1922–
    The challenge of world hunger / William Spencer
        p. cm. — (Environmental issues series)
    ISBN 0-89490-283-0
    1. Food supply. 2. Famines. 3. Famine relief. I. Title.
II. Series: Environmental issues series (Hillside, N.J.)
HD9000.5.S667 1991
363.8'83—dc20   90-49430
                                        CIP

Printed in the United States of America

10 9 8 7 6 5 4 3 2 1

Photo Credits:
Food and Agricultural Organization of the United Nations, pp. 4, 10, 11, 12, 16, 18, 20, 23, 25, 29, 31, 33, 40, 43, 45, 47, 49, 52.

Cover Photo:
Food and Agricultural Organization of the United Nations.

Contents

1 Hunger and People 5

2 The Science of Food Production 14

3 Technology and Food 26

4 Food Production and Politics 44

Glossary 57

Further Reading 59

For Further Information 61

Index 63

About the Author 64

A mother holds her child, already severely affected by malnutrition, at a refugee camp in the Begemder region of Ethiopia.

1

Hunger and People

A boy crawled from a mud-and-wattle hut and tried to stand, but his thin legs wouldn't support him, and he fell. His head was very large for his body, and his curly hair had receded as if he were an old man. When his mother picked him up, his spindly legs wrapped like vines around the sagging skin on her stomach. Amid a cluster of huts nearby, a girl stood silent, staring blankly, her skin stretched taut over her rib cage, pelvis, hipbones. Her knees stuck out like knots on a sapling.

This scene took place in Abyei, a village in the southern part of the Sudan, Africa's largest country, in October 1988. Earlier that year thousands of families had fled to Abyei from their homes in other villages to escape a savage civil war between Sudanese government troops and rebel soldiers. Most of these families had no food and no clothes except the rags on their backs. The war (which is still going on) had destroyed their villages, and relief organizations such as the Red Cross and Catholic Relief Services were prevented from delivering food supplies to Abyei and other refugee areas by government troops. The refugees were caught in the middle, between the government forces and the rebels, trapped without food or even drinking water.

What does it mean to go hungry not just for a few hours but for days, weeks, even months? Children such as those in Abyei can tell us. Hunger draws the skin drum tight across the bones. It makes old people (if they can walk at all) move with great care lest they fall, break a hip or a leg, and then lie on the ground until merciful death takes them away. Myles Harris, an American doctor working in refugee camps in Ethiopia in 1987, noted that constant hunger made parents no longer care for their thin, silent children. They would do anything, even betray their children, for the smallest mouthful of food.

Hunger in countries such as Sudan has become worse due to war, but throughout Africa it is increasing. More and more African countries are unable to feed their people and must import large amounts of grain and other food crops just to keep even with population growth. They often must borrow the funds needed to pay for these food imports from foreign banks or from rich countries, and thus go deeper and deeper into debt. But hunger is not limited to Africa or to any particular people in a particular time or place. The hungry can be found in every society, everywhere in the world where there is poverty, overcrowding, war, or other forms of human misery.

Sometimes hunger shows itself best in small human scenes. The Brazilian writer Maria de Jesus, who lived in one of the poorest slums of a large city, tells of an encounter with a boy in front of a garbage dump. Someone had thrown meat into the dump, and the boy was picking out the pieces. She warned him not to eat the meat—it was spoiled—but he would not listen to her. It was two days since he had had anything to eat, he told her. He ate the meat and went away. The next day she returned to the dump and found him there, dead from food poisoning. He was a pretty little boy, she wrote in her diary, but no one claimed him. He had no documents, and no one knew his name or had bothered to find out if he had a family.

Hunger can also be the result of natural causes such as crop failure. In Vietnam, a country ravaged by decades of war, seven million people faced starvation in 1988 because the rice crop failed. For the first time in Vietnamese history, country peasant women, their wide woven hats turned over as begging bowls, became a common sight on city streets.

Yet for many Americans, hunger is something we read about but seldom see in the course of our daily lives. We live in a land of plenty. Not only are the shelves of our supermarkets well stocked with the products of our farms, orchards, and food processing plants, but these shelves also display the foods of many other countries, all available if we are willing to pay the price. We are a generous people. When other countries are threatened with hunger and possible starvation, we respond generously with gifts of food and money. American schools usually provide a hot nutritious lunch for students during school days, and children can look forward to a refrigerator filled with food when they get home from school.

Does this mean that there are no hungry people here in the United States? Certainly not; disasters of various kinds strike American families as well as those elsewhere. When these things happen, people may go without food for a while. A parent loses a secure job when a factory or business closes or is forced to reduce its staff because of economic losses. A family member comes down with a serious illness, bringing with it huge medical bills. A fire puts a family out in the street in the dead of winter, its home destroyed, its possessions burned. If any of these things should happen to *your* family, one result could be that you might not know where your next meal was coming from.

Such misfortunes as these could happen to any family. But hunger of a different kind stalks even rich countries such as the United States in ever increasing numbers. More people go hungry for longer periods in these last decades of the twentieth century than ever before in our history. The Physicians' Task Force on Hunger in America reported in 1985 that 20 million Americans went hungry a good part of the year. In 1990 the number was 34 million, and one study reported that one out of eight children under the age of 12 was chronically under-nourished.

Hunger in America can mean not having a proper diet or enough of the right foods, or it can mean missing a meal or two every day. In Jackson County, Mississippi, a group of U.S. Congress members visiting a school asked some schoolgirls idling outside the building if they were glad to be out for the summer. "Oh no, sir," one of the girls replied. "Why not?" asked the Congress members in surprise. "Because when we is in school, we gets lunch," the girl explained. "In the summer we only gets supper."

A rural health nurse on the Navajo Indian reservation in New Mexico told a group of visiting doctors that "every year a few of our old people starve to death. Many of our reservation schools cannot give the children lunch because they can't afford the kitchen equipment required by the Bureau of Indian Affairs."

One way to measure the growth of hunger in our country is by the increase in the number of "soup kitchens," food banks, and food pantries that serve the poor and the hungry in our towns and cities. In the 1980s the number of these places skyrocketed. For example, New York City had 31 food pantries in 1981 compared with 600 in 1989! One food bank, Second Harvest, gives away on the average 387 *million* pounds (176 kilograms) of various foods every year!

Some people argue that the increase in places that give away free food actually proves that the hungry are being taken care of, that between food stamps, unemployment compensation, and food giveaways, no one really goes without food. However, a survey in Erie, Pennsylvania, which has one of the best emergency food systems in the country, found that 66 percent of persons served by the system (about 9 percent of the city's population) did not have enough food to get through the month and still needed emergency help. In Pennsylvania's second largest city, Pittsburgh, soup kitchens that usually serve 750 hungry people a day decided to hold an outdoor picnic for the poor in a public park one hot August day, and 1,500 people showed up for the free food.

Another reason that the extent of hunger is difficult to measure is because it wears many disguises and often goes unrecognized. One of these disguises is malnutrition. Malnutrition means that even when people have food to eat, it does not include enough vitamins, minerals, and other nutrients necessary for a balanced diet. And without a balanced diet, the growth of children is stunted, the elderly fall victim more easily to the diseases of old age, and adults become incapable of sustained or productive work. Malnutrition may be seen readily in the faces and bodies of refugee children in Sudan and Ethiopia, but it is present in nearly all societies. As an example, children visiting a health clinic in New Hampshire showed the effects; their hair was thin and dull instead of thick and shiny as it is with well-nourished children. Also, their eyes contained no sparkle, and they had little energy.

Malnutrition can also come from having too much of one kind of food, what we would call an unbalanced diet. It may be the result of ignorance. Parents in poor societies or the poorer sections of the population will often give their children foods that are high in starches and sugars. These foods are easier to prepare, they are more filling, and they cost less and do not spoil or rot as quickly as do the fresh vegetables and fruits needed to balance the diet. Children from poor families may appear to be well fed, even fat and healthy. But without a balanced and nutritious diet, they often have little energy. Thus, children tested in a village in Guatemala, Central America, where the diet is almost entirely of plant origin (black beans, corn, and potatoes), had energy levels 15 percent to 25 percent lower than the normal levels set by the World Health Organization. Their diet was high in protein, but it lacked the carbohydrates needed to give them the right amount of energy.

In addition to loss of energy, a poor diet allows diseases caused by dietary deficiencies to become common among certain groups.

Scurvy, caused by a lack of vitamin C in the diet, used to be common among sailors at sea because their diet lacked citrus fruit. Captains who docked their ships at ports where oranges, grapefruit, lemons, or limes could be bought found out that scurvy was cured when these fruits were given to their crews. Similarly, rickets, a common childhood disease in the United States earlier in the twentieth century, was discovered to be caused by a lack of Vitamin D. Children in areas where the winters are long or where there is a great deal of fog (such as coastal Washington state) were more affected than those in sunny areas, and black children more than whites (because their darker skin color blocks out the sunlight). But as was the case with scurvy, the addition of a missing vitamin to the diet largely wiped out the disease.

The side effects of malnutrition are particularly severe among

A girl and her young sister live on a farm in northeast Brazil. Note the younger girl's swollen abdomen, the result of poor nutrition.

rural populations, due not only to poor diet but also to ignorance and overpopulation. Thomas Bass, an American scientist and writer who traveled widely in Africa in 1989–90, observed village children literally wasting away from marasmus, a disease he says is caused by "a double dose of malnutrition from lack of calories and protein in their diet." Kwashiorkor, meaning "the sickness that comes to the first child after the second is born," is common in rural African families where the birth of a child deprives its next-oldest sibling of his or her mother's milk, so that he or she must fend for himself or herself from the family food pot. The United Nations Children's Fund (UNICEF), which is concerned with the health of children all over the world, has tried to help cut down the effect of this disease by discouraging the use of cassava, a food plant which is common in Africa. The plant is cheap and easy to grow, but unfortunately it has little food value. An

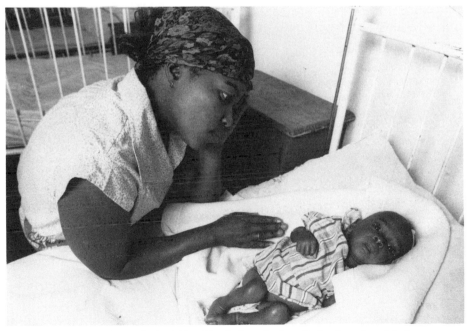

A young mother at the bedside of her baby, who is suffering from kwashiorkor.

American Baptist missionary told Bass, "Any food is better than cassava. It keeps you alive until measles or diarrhea comes along."

Thus, malnutrition alone is not usually fatal to people, either adults or children. It is the diseases that develop as a result of hunger and malnutrition that cause most deaths—especially among children. Myles Harris, an American doctor, describes vividly the effects of kwashiorkor on children in an Ethiopian refugee camp: "Their hair fell out, and what was left turned slightly red. Their bellies swelled, then their legs, then their faces. In mockery of health their skins took on the shiny gleaming look that gave them the name of 'sugar babies.' "

As we begin the 1990s, UNICEF estimates that without great improvements to their diet some 13 to 18 million children a year will die either directly from starvation or indirectly from malnutrition-related illnesses. In some parts of the world this adds up to 40,000 children a day. Even as you read this page, several hundred persons a

Transplanting rice on a new field which has been cleared by deforestation.

day are dying needlessly—poor, hungry, and perhaps, nameless like the Brazilian boy in Maria de Jesus' diary.

Most experts agree that we have the resources and the technology needed to end hunger in the world. But hunger is not a simple problem. It cannot be ended merely by providing food for people who need it, without changing their diet, their customs, their agriculture, even their way of life. Hunger is affected by food production methods, by population growth, by agricultural practices, and by environmental misuse. Lester Brown warns us in the new book *State of the World 1990* that increasing world output in the 1990s to meet expected demands will be difficult, due to the growing lack of farmland and water resources and the effects of global warming, climate change, cutting down of forests, and other forms of environmental misuse.

In the next chapters of this book we will look at hunger problems in terms of how science and technology can affect food production. The last chapter is concerned with "the politics of food," or how political actions by governments affect people's food needs. Modern science can, and does, help Mother Nature in improving food crops and bringing a steady supply of food to our dinner tables. Technology uses new engineering processes and scientific discoveries to develop disease-free varieties of crops. The most advanced form of technology is biotechnology, the key to a future in which we may soon have the perfect potato, the perfect bean, as scientists unlock the secrets of plant life and actually change the genetic structure of food crops. Yet, science and technology are only two parts of the world food production system; they must depend upon the humans who now sit at the controls of our planet managing its environment while trying to protect it for future use.

2

The Science of Food Production

The need for food and, in particular, the need to have an adequate balanced diet are basic human needs. Without food people cannot survive, and without an adequate diet they may survive but are more likely to grow up as weaklings, inferior in physical if not mental ability to their better-fed neighbors. The great importance of food in our lives suggests that it is not only a basic human need, but also a right. From the beginning of time, people have fought to deprive others of the lands needed for food production, through war or conquest, the stronger driving out the weaker.

Food may be a human right, but to have enough food people must have the ability either to grow it or buy it. Most people today do not grow the foods they eat, and they live far away from the farms that grow their food. Today most of our food is packaged, shipped to city markets, distributed, and sold before it reaches our dinner tables. Our food delivery system costs money all along the way, from the farmer's income to the wages of his workers, to shipping, and to marketing and distribution costs as each person or business in the system takes a share of the profits.

Agriculture

Agriculture is the scientific cultivation of the earth for food. It dates back some 10,000 years—a relatively short period in the evolution of the human species. It was probably first practiced in the area we today call the Middle East by scattered groups living in Mesopotamia (modern Iraq) and Turkey. These early peoples learned by trial and error how to cultivate the soil, to find edible weeds, and experiment with wild plants until they could grow enough food crops to feed themselves and their families.

The Role of Climate

These early farmers were dependent upon sun, wind, and rain to grow their crops. In many parts of the world, food production still requires that these factors are favorable. Computer measurements and satellite photography, along with simulated weather models, tell us (most of the time) what the weather is going to be for any given period. But they do not tell us how to control the climate nor how it is likely to change due to human actions such as pollution. Too little rain —or too much—wind, dust, and atmospheric changes such as the "greenhouse effect" all affect agriculture, and therefore, food production.

Weather is not exactly the same as climate. Weather affects food production in the short term, in the sequence of the seasons, the planting, tending, and harvesting of crops. Climate is long term, affecting our lives over many years, even centuries.

In terms of its effect on world food production, one of the most serious climatic problems is drought. Drought is the lack of rainfall over a particular period of time. Many areas in the world are affected by cycles of drought. The Sahel, a region just south of the Sahara desert in Africa, populated by nomad tribes, had almost no rainfall from the 1960s to the late 1980s. The nomads lost most of their livestock and had to move into cities to survive. Georgia, an important American agricultural state, had a severe drought in 1987–88, and many farms that had been owned by the same families for generations had to be sold as their owners gave up farming. The wheat crop in Kansas, which is essential to world grain stocks, was 30 percent below normal in 1989 due to dust storms that blew dry Kansas soil all the way to Chicago!

Sometimes climatic changes that affect food production happen in different places at the same time. In 1972 heat and lack of rain in Russia ruined the wheat crop, while the monsoon rains that make food crops possible in India arrived late and ended earlier than usual, reducing harvests by two-thirds. In Peru, a shift in ocean currents in the same year sharply reduced the catch of anchovies, a small fish that is the country's principal export as well as the main source of protein in the Peruvian diet. Due to these climatic changes, total world food production dropped by 2 percent.

Soils and Soil Fertility

The soil that covers the surface of our earth is one of our most

A close up of the cracked surface of dried mud near Paratinga, Brazil.

important natural resources. Not only our food, but also indirectly our shelter, clothing, and other necessities come from the ground under out feet. But often we have not used this ground wisely in our efforts to obtain these essentials. Many great civilizations of the past have disappeared or collapsed due to misuse of the land and its resources. One example is the Mayan civilization of Central America. The Mayas ruled a powerful empire more than 1,000 years ago. But as the Mayan population grew, more and more forests were cut down and burned, with food crops planted in the burned areas. But with the trees gone, the soil was washed away by rains, and the land grew less and less food until people began starving to death. Countries such as Nepal, Madagascar, and Brazil are misusing their forests and soils in the same way today and can probably expect the same results.

Good, rich topsoil is essential to food crops. But originally all soil was rock. Over millions of years this rock was crumbled into fine dust by sun, wind, and water. Topsoil, which is different from crumbled rock, is formed by the addition of organic matter, such as leaves, animal remains, rotting fruits and vegetables, and wild plants, which falls into the soil and is slowly dissolved. This process makes the soil rich by adding important nutrients. In areas such as deserts, where there is little organic matter in the soil, there is not much topsoil, and consequently less food can be grown, although some desert soils or even sand (which has no organic matter) can be used to grow food crops.

Good soil, Robert Howard tells us, is like good skin: it is healthy, air and water circulate through it, and organic matter adds the right balance of vitamins, nutrients, and minerals. The world's best natural soils are found in valleys and bottom lands fed by silt-carrying rivers, such as the Nile Delta in Egypt. African soils are among the poorest, mostly made from kaolin clay and rock that are quickly eroded by wind and sun into a surface as hard as concrete. It is a constant struggle for African farmers to make their soil produce food for them, and explains in part why a continent that was self-sufficient in food production until the 1960s must now import most of its food.

Irrigation

Irrigation is the use of water by man-made rather than natural methods to nourish crops. The main reason for irrigation is to provide water to crops on a regular basis in areas where rainfall is rare. Farmers have developed many different irrigation systems over the years. They have dug wells, diverted rivers into smaller streams brought to their fields through a network of pipes, or built underground pipelines that carry water downhill from distant mountaintops by gravity flow.

There is plenty of water on the surface of the earth, but this water is unevenly distributed. Almost 97 percent is salt water, locked away in the oceans. The remaining 3 percent is fresh water, which we use for washing, drinking, energy, and other human needs, in addition to

Siphoning water from an irrigation canal to cultivate the fields in the Itiquis River Basin of Costa Rica.

food production. About two-thirds goes to agriculture. Since we have so little fresh water, efficient use is essential to produce the food and energy required by the earth's growing human population.

Irrigation use has greatly increased in this century. About 497 million acres, one-seventh of the total area that is presently used to grow food, are irrigated. Five countries—the United States, China, India, the Soviet Union, and Pakistan—have the largest amount of irrigated land. However, some of the world's most productive cultivated areas make relatively little use of irrigation for crops. Farmers in the U.S. "Corn Belt," which extends from western Ohio across Indiana, Illinois, and Iowa to Nebraska and Missouri, usually have been able to count on adequate rainfall, rich soil, and the large amount of land available for farming to produce the largest harvest of wheat, corn, soybeans, and other grains in human history.

Putting the Land to Work

Good food production depends upon the efforts of the producer as much as it does upon nature; it takes human hands to start the process. The soil must be tilled or worked over, seeds sown, water and drainage supplied, and fertilizers and other nutrients added to nourish the soil as the growing plants use up the nutrients already there. As the growth cycle moves toward harvest, weeds must be controlled and plants watched carefully for insect pests and the diseases they may bring with them. Farmers must also keep a wary eye upon the sky for rainfall and other weather changes that might affect the crops. A good farmer, like a good gardener, is a genius at knowing the particular patch of earth he works with—its soil, its water resources, the weather patterns of his area—and he works with a high degree of professional skill to use his patches in the best possible way to produce food for many people besides himself and his family.

Farmers today depend upon technology and modern equipment along with fertilizers, pesticides, and improved seeds developed in laboratories to put the land to work. But science and technology do not necessarily guarantee better and more abundant crops. Five hundred or so years ago, the Incas, a people who ruled over a large empire in South America, developed a system of agriculture well suited to their land. Their empire stretched from the hot, wet jungles of the Amazon River and its basin to the lower slopes of the Andes Mountains to the 15,000-foot heights of the High Andes—covering three different climate zones. In each zone they planted food crops that would grow well in that particular zone. Using simple tools, they cut stone blocks and fitted them together to make a series of terraces down the mountainsides and dug canals lined with other blocks to bring water down from the melting Andes snows to irrigate their crops. The Incas developed many new varieties of food plants, including potatoes that would grow at 15,000-foot altitudes, twenty kinds of corn, and other crops rich in protein. When the Spanish destroyed the Inca empire, they also ruined the Inca system of agriculture. Until very

Terraces have been used for centuries to prevent erosion in cultivated hilly regions.

recently most of these food plants, which can be grown in other parts of the world to help solve the hunger problem, were forgotten.

Misusing the Environment

The Incas practiced what we would call sustainable agriculture—that is, they worked *with* nature rather than *against* it, maintaining and improving the environment to grow better food crops. But today many nations are more concerned with increasing food production to feed their growing populations than with keeping a balance between people and nature. Poor countries prefer growing food crops that are exported to improving the food supply for their own people. In many countries people are moving into cities from the country at a very fast rate, while cities spread out into the countryside, often taking over the best farmland for new suburbs and housing developments. As a result, there is less and less land on which to grow food crops and fewer farmers to work the land.

In terms of the science of food production, the most serious problem we face is the misuse not only of farmland but also the earth's environment. Many scientists believe that our industrial society, with its huge demands for food, fuel, water, and air, is using up natural resources so fast that within a century the earth will be unliveable for humans and animals. The writer Bill McKibben tells us that we are no longer part of nature: "What began with our changing of the atmosphere and has continued with genetic engineering—changing the structure of plants and animals to improve them—will end a relationship that has lasted for millions of years. Now nature is part of a universe ruled by man."

Deforestation

The cutting down of trees without either replacing them or letting them grow to full height and then cutting selectively (which is good forestry practice) is called deforestation. It is one of the most serious misuses of the environment. Trees are important to food production because they lower temperatures in the area around them, provide protection for crops and livestock from the blazing sun in the summer, and help the soil retain water. But all over the world trees are being cut down faster than they can replaced. Senator Albert Gore, Jr., noted recently that each year the trees in an area the size of his home state of Tennessee disappear under the axes and power saws of loggers. The most serious deforestation is in the tropical rain forests. This is especially unfortunate because these rain forests have little value to food production, but are extremely important to our world's weather and climate and the preservation of many species of plants and animals. In countries with vast rain forests like Brazil, the government encourages poor families from cities to move into the forest areas and cut down the trees in order to plant food crops and become self-sufficient. In other countries timber is the only fuel available, as in Haiti (where it is used to make charcoal), or the only export crop, as in Laos. Laos, a small Asian country, has been cutting down its forests to export wood to Thailand, its next-door neighbor. Thailand does not have as many forests as Laos and prohibits logging in them, meanwhile encouraging Laos to cut down *its* trees.

A problem related to deforestation is erosion. This happens when trees are cut down and wind and rain wash the soil into the sea or down the mountainsides, leaving the earth open to the baking sun. Madagascar, an island republic off the east coast of Africa, provides a good example of this problem. A century ago the island was covered with tropical forests, the habitat of many animals and plants found nowhere else on earth. At that time Madagascar had a small population, but today there are 11 million people in a land one and a half times the size of California. Their needs for fuel and building materials have caused all but a tiny part of the rain forests to be cut down. And with the forests gone, there is nothing to hold the good soil in place when the rains come; the island is literally washing into the ocean. At this rate Madagascar will become a desert in the twenty-first century. How will it feed its people? No one knows.

Desertification

The spread of deserts, called desertification, is another important example of the misuse of the environment that affects food production. To some extent this is a natural process. The Sahara desert in Africa is expanding at the rate of 3.6 miles (6 kilometers) a year over the croplands along its northern and southern borders. In other parts of the world, the same thing is happening; the United Nations estimated in 1983 that 35 percent of the earth's surface is threatened with desertification. But human misuse of the land is a major cause. Deforestation, overuse of underground water supplies for irrigation, and overgrazing of sparse pasturelands by cattle all contribute to the unnecessary spread of deserts.

Intensive gully erosion in the Sakay region of Madagascar. Deforestation has caused the erosion of valuable topsoil.

The overuse of water resources also affects food production. The Aral Sea, in Soviet central Asia, is actually a large inland freshwater lake. It was formerly full of fish, and the fishing industry there was very important to the Soviet economy. But in recent years large amounts of its water were drawn off to irrigate cotton fields along its shores, Soviet agricultural experts having learned that cotton would grow well in the hot, humid climate of central Asia. As a result, the Aral Sea has shrunk to 40 percent of its former size. Its largest fishing port is now 30 miles (48 kilometers) from the water. Irrigation made possible a 400 percent increase in Soviet cotton production. But cotton expansion spelled the end of the fishing industry. Fish will no longer live in the Aral Sea due to its high concentration of salt, fertilizer draining off from the cotton fields, and chemical pesticides that do not break down in its water.

Similar water problems affect some of our western states, where water resources are also scarce. In the San Luis Valley of Colorado, a semidesert area where rainfall averages 7 inches (18 centimeters) a year, the discovery of an underground water source, called an *aquifer*, in 1986 set off a battle between farmers and developers. The farmers needed the water to irrigate their food crops and nourish their live- stock, while the developers wanted to drill wells for homeowners in the new subdivisions they planned to build. One water company even proposed pumping out as much as 6.5 billion gallons of water a year to sell to thirsty cities like Denver! The Colorado state government in this case sided with the farmers and ranchers and in 1989 blocked all further valley development and took the case to court. Depending on the outcome of the court case, the valley will either become an area of subdivisions or remain a farming area important to food production and more important, a source of water for thirsty Coloradoans!

What are the prospects for the world's food supply in the coming years? Lester Brown, who directs the Worldwatch Institute, a Washington, D.C.-based organization that is concerned with all the

problems of our environment, human and natural—feels that the prospects are not good. And many scientists agree with him. In the Institute's annual "State of the World" report, Brown reports that the growth of the world's population, the loss of forests, the destruction of the ozone layer above the earth (the "greenhouse effect," which seems to be causing significant climatic changes in various areas), the overuse of water for nonagricultural purposes, and other examples of human mistreatment of the environment will cause a drop in the production of food. If this assessment is correct, the result will be that millions of people will suffer from serious malnutrition if not famine. But given the problem-solving skills of human beings and the extraordinary development of science in this century, such a result may not happen. If it does not, one reason will be the improvements in food production due to technology, which we will examine in the next chapter.

Men and women plant tree seedlings to prevent sand dune formation in Vietnam.

25

3

Technology and Food

The word *technology* comes from the Greek *techne*, meaning an art or skill. The ancient Greek runners and athletes who performed in the first Olympic Games practiced *techne*. So did the artists who left their monuments in stone in temples, statues, and busts of the Greek gods. But in recent years technology has come to be used to describe various fields of science and engineering, including the science of food. There is an "art" of food preparation that consists of using the right ingredients and the skill of cooks to create delicious and attractive meals. But there is also a science or technology of food that uses scientific principles of nutrition in the preparation of foods, and engineering principles in the growing of the crops that provide that food.

The basic tools of technology have been developed over a long time through a process of cultural evolution. Cultural evolution is different from biological evolution. Biological evolution is a very slow process. Changes in the biological makeup of living creatures take millions of years, and some species have changed hardly at all since prehistoric times. Earlier species, such as the dinosaurs, probably became extinct because their biological nature could not adapt to changes in their environment. Others, such as horses, birds, and most

of all human beings, have adapted more successfully to environmental changes and are still here on earth.

Biological evolution affects all living creatures and is an on-going process, despite its slowness. Cultural evolution, in contrast, goes on at a much faster rate. It may be defined as the sum total of the ways of life of particular societies, groups, or living species, and the methods each group or species uses to improve its way of life. For example, squirrels have learned how to open acorns with their claws, and vultures in Egypt have learned to drop eggs taken from the nests of other birds onto rocks to break the shells and get at the protein inside.

However, these examples of the cultural evolution of certain living species are mainly improvements in food collection and use. They do not compare with the cultural evolution of the human species. Human cultural evolution is not only superior to that of other living creatures, it is the only one that threatens the environment of the whole earth. Nature has always put biological limits on the animal world; predators such as lions and tigers kill only to meet their food needs, as do grass-eating animals in the wild. The biologist David Barash writes: "Only man is actually dangerous to the environment that provides our food, shelter, air and water," and sad to say, he is right. Once we were part of nature, a unit of the natural world along with the trees, rivers, birds, animals, the land, and the vast sky that holds sway over our heads. But humans have never been satisfied until they could rule this natural world—and now the mountains that rise above us are ringed, not with natural clouds but with clouds of soot, sulfur, carbon dioxide, and other human pollutants from our homes, factories, and cars. The naturalist Bill McKibben warns that by changing nature we have brought an end to the world of nature, substituting for it a world that meets our needs. For example, dams on a Canadian river bring electricity to Canadian homes; but caribou crossing the river on their annual migration drown because their usual crossing-point is now a huge sheet of water. An environment productive only for people is not the same as a natural one.

The human species also differs from other living species in social and technological development. Social evolution refers to changes in governments, legal systems, family organization, divisions of work, and group relations of human society. Technological evolution consists of the inventions, tools, machines, and so on that have enabled us to develop our culture and eventually to dominate the natural world around us. Technological evolution is much faster that social evolution. The democracy of today is not much better than the Greek democratic system of several thousand years ago. But technology, based upon science, has drastically changed both our culture and the environment in which we live.

For most of human history, technology was a simple process of developing special tools to meet the changing needs of society. The woven baskets of Indian peoples, hand axes, the wheel, weaving loom, pottery, bows and arrows, and animal-drawn plow were all technological tools invented or modified to make life a bit easier for humankind. But in the late twentieth century technology has come to mean "hi-tech," that is, the latest developments in microchips, computers, satellite photography, and so on.

One important difference between the technological evolution of today and that of past centuries is that in many societies, particularly in the industrial countries, people live and work far away from their food production sources. Susanna Langer, a philosopher at Harvard University, once wrote of the typical city dweller that "seedtime and harvest are nothing to him. His realities are the motors that run elevators, subway trains, and cars, the crates of foodstuffs that arrive by night." Our isolation from the natural environment makes us indifferent to the fact that we often misuse it, and even in poorer countries, where people still live close to their food sources, population pressure forces these people to misuse it for their own selfish purposes. In Nepal, Brazil, Haiti, and many other nonindustrial countries, the struggle to survive has led people to do serious damage to their environment.

Yet, there is a bright side to technology. We humans now have not only the tools, but also often the motivation to protect and even improve the environment to ensure human survival. Unlike biological evolution, technological evolution comes out of action by the human brain. It is not an on-going natural process; human thought and effort must work to keep it going. Improved food production through technology and development of new varieties of food plants (or the rediscovery of forgotten food plants such as "blue corn" and amaranth) offers some hope that we can work with nature rather than against it to ensure the survival of the earth as a livable planet for all creatures, great or small.

In some parts of the world, primitive methods of agriculture that rely on animal power are still used. This farmer plows a paddy field in Pakistan.

Old and New Technologies

Food production has benefited from a number of technological developments, some scientifically new, others being the "rediscovery" of old and proven agricultural methods or food sources. These developments include the "Green Revolution," alternative farming methods and practices that do not misuse the environment, organic farming, and the wider distribution of locally grown food plants with high nutritional value to reduce both hunger and malnutrition. Perhaps the most exciting development in food production is the new field of biotechnology, the changing of plant and animal genetic structures to improve crops, and thus increase the total food supply.

The Green Revolution

The first "Green Revolution" took place about 10,000 years ago in the Middle East, and at the same time in central Africa when people discovered they could grow certain edible wild plants. Ten thousand years later a second Green Revolution was set off by the development of hybrid wheat, corn, and rice plants that grow better and produce bigger harvests than do the ordinary varieties of these plants. Dr. Norman Borlaug, a Kansas farm boy who grew up to become a scientist, developed such a hybrid wheat plant by crossing several kinds of wheat. Borlaug's hybrid plant was smaller than the wheat we see waving in the breeze on American farms. Because of its small size, the plant could absorb large amounts of fertilizer, and as a result, it produced three times as much wheat as the larger plants.

Other scientists using similar methods were able to develop hybrid corn plants, and in the 1960s a miniature rice plant was developed that would better stand heat and drought than ordinary rice plants and produce twice the rice. When these new plants were distributed, many people felt that they would bring about "revolutionary" changes in food production, hence the term "Green Revolution." The impact of the new discoveries was greatest in poor countries, where rapid

Giant wheat originated by crossing
different strains of Mexican wheat.

A "super" variety of rice that
produces much greater yields.

population growth, along with lack of rainfall and other problems, made it especially hard for governments to meet food needs. India became self-sufficient in wheat by 1972, and South Korea and Taiwan, both Asian countries where rice is important in the diet, greatly increased their rice harvest. One reason was that the hybrid rice plants had a shorter growing season, 105 days as opposed to 200 for standard rice varieties, so that rice planters now could harvest two crops a year with irrigation.

It seemed to many people in the 1970s that the Green Revolution was like a miracle; it would automatically solve the world's food problems. Farmers just had to keep on planting the hybrid plants and food production would keep up with population growth. But it has not worked out that way. Population growth continues to accelerate, and urbanization, the movement of rural people into cities, has seriously affected agriculture through loss of workers and conversion of farmland to housing projects. Also, many governments have invested in industries at the expense of agricultural development. David Cusack notes that fifty African, Asian, and Latin American countries that were formerly self-sufficient in food must now import wheat and other food crops to feed their populations.

The Green Revolution "super plants" need larger amounts of fertilizer than ordinary varieties. Although many farmers in the poor countries use the fertilizer nutrients efficiently, they cannot afford to buy all the fertilizers that are needed. (Almost all the fertilizer and pesticides used in these countries must be imported, as very little of either product is produced locally.)

The Green Revolution varieties have also proved to be more affected by changes in weather or climate than ordinary varieties. In addition, heavy use of fertilizers and pesticides has caused health problems in some areas, while nitrogen run-off from fertilized fields has polluted some lakes and rivers. Also, although employment is higher in Green Revolution areas due to the large number of workers required to water, tend, and harvest the crops, the higher costs of production have forced many small farmers in poor countries out of business. Many farm families in these areas have been forced to migrate to the cities, adding to urban overpopulation and other problems.

Agriculture in the Industrial Countries

Food production in most industrial nations is much better organized and more efficient and productive than it is in the developing countries of Asia, Africa, and Latin America. Most farms and ranches in Western Europe and the United States are well managed and yield bountiful harvests. Probably the world's most productive farm system is the American one, and its success is due in large part to the use of

Farmers in Nigeria using fertilizers to increase yam crop yields.

technology. The World Commission on Environment and Development, a United Nations advisory group, reported in 1983 that during the period 1950–83 the world's population grew from 2.51 billion to 4.66 billion, but food production during the same period increased by 900 million tons. If this increase had been distributed evenly throughout the world, it would have meant that each person's food intake increased from 547 pounds (248 kilograms) to 686 pounds (311 kilograms) per year. The greatest increase in production was in the United States because of our large use of fertilizers, pesticides, and machines.

However, overuse of technology for food production sometimes leads to bad results in terms of the effect on croplands or on public health. The mucklands of southern Florida are the number one source of winter vegetables for the entire country; sugarcane is this state's second or third highest money-earning crop; and the north-central Florida town of Hastings advertises itself, with good reason, as the cabbage and potato capital of the state! But these crops require enormous amounts of fertilizers and pesticides due to Florida's humid climate and its hordes of plant pests. By the 1980s the millions of people flocking to Florida for work, vacation, or retirement discovered that the chemical fertilizers and sprays used on these crops for business reasons were affecting the air they breathed, the water they drank or swam in, and worst of all, the conditions under which migrant workers in the croplands had to work.

Too much use of chemicals in food production has affected public health in many other parts of the United States. In October 1988 the Environmental Protection Agency (EPA) reported that 252 of the 360 chemical ingredients in the pesticides most commonly used on food crops may cause cancer in humans. Dean Kleckner, president of the American Farm Bureau Federation and an Iowa farmer, told a reporter recently that "thirty years ago when I began farming I would dump my insecticides on my corn and stand downwind so that the fumes blew back in my face. That's dangerous, but I didn't know it. And I don't think the chemical companies knew it either." Today alarm bells are ringing not only here, but also around the world as more and more chemicals are suspected of causing cancer—including those that have been used for years in pesticides. In May 1989 the EPA banned the use of Alar, a chemical sprayed on apples to keep them fresh and crisp, after tests on rats showed evidence of the growth of cancer cells.

Biotechnology and Food Production

If the Green Revolution seems to have run out of steam, what new forms of technology might come along to keep food production increasing as populations grow? The evidence of scarcity is frightening. Drought in the key grain-producing countries, in particular the United States, in 1987–88 resulted in poor harvests; grain stockpiles, essential for shipment to many poor countries, reached their lowest level in years. The 1989 harvest was 18 million tons short despite good weather and higher prices paid to farmers by the government under the grain subsidy program. Lester Brown warns in the Institute's newest book that "growth in world food output is being slowed by environmental misuse, scarcity of farmland and water for irrigation, and less success in the effectiveness of chemical fertilizers in improving output." Meanwhile, the earth's population is growing by 90 million a year. Food production would have to be increased by 28 million tons a year just to feed these new people. Biotechnology is not a new field. Its basic principles have been known and used for thousands of years. Noah used them to make wine from grapes to celebrate the landing of the ark on dry ground. He must have understood something about the principles that go into winemaking. Some 4,000 years ago people were making bread with the aid of yeast, which causes it to rise through a simple fermentation process. Fermentation, the simplest form of biotechnology, results from the action of leaven (yeast) on dough or on liquids containing sugar, as when grapes are compressed. As a result, their natures are changed by a chemical process.

What *is* new about biotechnology is the great increase in the last fifty years in our understanding of the structure of living organisms. The discovery of DNA, the chemical molecule that determines the genetic character of an organism, was the first step. DNA, the abbreviation for deoxyribonucleic acid, is found in living organisms in the form of two long chains of cells that twist around each other in a helix or spiral. The way the chains are paired determines the organisms's genetic structure. An understanding of DNA and its function in making protein (the substance necessary to nourish life) has enabled scientists to make discoveries that have begun to change our lives.

Norman Borlaug believes, as do many scientists, that the greatest contributions of biotechnology to our lives are likely to be in the fields of medicine and health, animal sciences, and microbiology. "It will take much longer," he says, "to develop techniques that will dramatically improve production of our major food crops." Since more is known about the basic cell processes of animals than of plants, scientists already are able to increase animal weight (or milk production) though hormones that speed up growth. In recent years, more and more companies have gone into the "genetic engineering" business, primarily to make a profit rather than to advance the cause of scientific research. Peering into the future, one writer promises us chickens without heads, feathers, or wings, since biotechnology's purpose is to provide the maximum amount of chicken meat for our dinner tables. Chickens will no longer be recognized as such, but as hunks of flesh!

More fortunate for the plant than the chicken, it is difficult to change genes in plants in order to grow better food crops. Cereals are particularly resistant to genetic change. One important discovery in the field of biotechnology that may help to increase food production involves the "fixing" of nitrogen in plants. Nitrogen, which is found both in the air and the soil, is the essential chemical element needed to develop the protein and other natural nutrients within cells that make life possible. Nearly 80 percent of the air we breathe is made up of nitrogen gas. However, this nitrogen, because it exists in the form of gas, is useless to most forms of life. Animals get the nitrogen they need for growth from eating plants or other animals, but plants must get it from the soil.

Some plants have the ability to "fix" or replace the nitrogen used in making food crops, while other plants use up nitrogen and do not replace it (so that the lost amounts are returned to the soil). For example, farmers have known for years that planting legume crops (beans, peas, clover) in fields previously planted in wheat or corn restores the fertility of the soil. The reason is that millions of tiny organisms called bacteria live in the roots of these crops and fix nitrogen from the air into the soil. However, wheat, corn, and rice, the most important crops in terms of the world food supply, do not fix nitrogen in the soil. Experiments to develop a hybrid wheat or rice plant that will fix nitrogen in the soil have shown good results in laboratory tests, but we need to know much more about plant structure before nitrogen-fixing, disease-resistant, pest-free food crops are ready for the farmer.

Genetic engineering is responsible for the growing numbers of gene banks, not only in the industrial countries, but also in the poorer nations. A gene bank is a "bank" in that things are received and stored there as savings or deposits, but instead of money these "things" are plant seeds. High in the Andes Mountains of Colombia, a gene bank has been set up to store more than sixty different kinds of potatoes carrying the disease-resistant genes of the ancient high-altitude potato grown by the Incas. If you were to visit Bogota, the Colombian capital, you would see many of these potatoes. Some of them are yellow and shaped like tennis balls, others like dumplings, and still others like sausages or oddly shaped carrots. You would not think of them as potatoes, but they have tremendous possibilities for the world's food supply.

However, not everyone agrees that "designer gene" plants are safe even though they may help improve the food supply. The Ecological Society of America, a group concerned about the plants' possible effects upon the environment, warned in a 1989 report in its magazine *Ecology* that we still do not know enough about the long-term effects on the environment of planting "gene-tailored" crops, whereas the effects of releasing chemicals is well known. As an example of attempts to improve food crops genetically, a California company in 1987 began spraying strawberry plants with Frostban, a product it had developed by combining certain frost-resistant bacteria with bacteria from the strawberry plants. By adding the frost-resistant bacteria to the plants, the company hoped to lengthen their growing season and cut down on crop losses from frost. The verdict is not yet in on Frostban, but as these techniques improve we may see rice plants that thrive in brackish water (part fresh, part salt), frost-free tomatoes, and even headless and wingless chickens that still squawk!

Alternative Methods of Agriculture

Many aspects of biotechnology are still unknown; they belong to the realm of science fiction. Scientists are just beginning to understand photosynthesis—the process that changes carbon dioxide into oxygen and sugars by combining chlorophyll, a green pigment, with the sun's energy to bring about the growth of green plants. Sometimes a technological "breakthrough" brings with it new mysteries. Why is it, for example, that some of the microbes on the roots of nitrogen-fixing plants are killers, causing diseases such as root rot or wilt in these plants, while others nourish the plants? Thus far the answer to that mystery has eluded researchers.

However, there are practical alternatives to high-cost genetic engineering that will certainly increase the food supply if used. One such alternative is to use foods that were important to people for their nutritional value but were no longer consumed as similar foods with less nutritional value became popular. Bread is a good example. In many countries bread was usually made from millet, sorghum, and other coarse grains. It was dark and heavy in texture, but very nutritious. However, in the last half-century, white bread made from imported wheat flour has replaced coarse dark bread in these countries. The problem is that in making white bread the germ and bran—the main sources of fiber, protein, and other nutrients—are removed. The flour is then bleached to make it white. Even when it is enriched with additives, only a few of the lost nutrients are put back into the bread. Eating white bread gave social status to poor people but did not improve their diet.

A simpler way to improve the food supply would be the wider use of food plants that grow well in one area of the world but not in other areas. However, many of these plants can be grown easily in other areas that have similar climate and soil conditions. The moringa—called the "vegetable tree" because its leaves are edible when cooked, thrives in the thin soils of tropical Latin America but can be grown wherever similar conditions exist. Pigeon peas, a bush plant grown in the Caribbean countries, has double value as a food resource because its fruit is edible with a high protein value, and after five years the bushes die and can be used for firewood.

The winged bean, first grown in New Guinea, is a tropical vine that grows well in humid climates and in all types of soil, however poor they are. The leaves, flowers, and fruit are all edible, and in terms of nutritional value it is similar to soybeans, but is easier to grow—requiring only a small investment by farmers.

Low Technology Systems
Agricultural systems that use little energy and natural materials, which seem almost to spring out of the environment, are another alternative

to high technology farming. One example is a system developed by a Swiss group to use biogas (organic material fermented by bacteria in tanks to form sludge for natural fertilizer) as a food source for certain algae found in African lakes. After fermentation the biogas is drawn through clean water that "bubbles off" the carbon dioxide generated by the fermenting process. The carbon dioxide solution is then fed to the algae, and nitrogen is added to make them edible. The system is completely integrated. The biogas generates methane for fuel, the fish in the lakes feed on the algae, and people either eat the fish or harvest the algae as a food supplement for their babies.

Another low technology system involves aquaculture, which is the process of growing and harvesting food in water. It is very important to the world's food supply. Over 6 percent of the total protein diet of people comes from fish and other aquatic food products. In some countries in Africa fish accounts for 50 percent of the total animal protein in the diet.

In rural China, a woman is filling the family biogas unit. Biogas is made from human and animal excreta and organic matter fermented in airtight "digesters" to produce methane gas.

The usual form of aquaculture food systems is the fish farm. China is a world leader in model fish farms. The Chinese have been raising fish in ponds for 3,000 years. Fish farming came about because a Chinese emperor decreed that a popular species of carp could not be eaten. A resourceful engineer got around the problem by building a pond in which different species of carp were harvested according to their feeding preferences. The surface feeders came first, then those who fed on algae from the pond depths, then the bottom feeders who lived on nutrients in the muck at the bottom of the pond. Since all carp look pretty much alike, it was impossible for the emperor's spies to tell the prohibited carp from the others.

Modern Chinese fish farms are larger (one farm alone covers 18,000 acres) but not vastly different in operation. Maintenance costs are low, and yields are high. And as anyone knows who has "fished for his supper" from a pond stocked with trout, bass, or bream, there is no food dish quite as tasty or nutritious. Freshwater fish farming is also more dependable than ocean fishing, which is affected by weather, disputes over fishing rights between countries, and human disasters such as oil spills.

Perhaps the best alternative to biotechnology is the use of farming methods that work *with* nature rather than to control nature. A common term for these methods is sustainable agriculture. It refers to the methods used to preserve the environment, to "sustain" it, while improving techniques that increase food production.

What are some of these sustainable methods? They include crop rotation in place of monoculture (planting the same crop year after year in the same fields); planting cover crops such as legumes or grasses to restore fertility to the soil; the use of organic, rather than chemical, herbicides and pesticides; tree planting in dry or semidesert areas to protect food crops; and the use of organic fertilizers. An encouraging development for the world's food supply is that food growers in a number of countries are using these methods. Thus, in south Florida vegetable growers have begun to change from chemical to organic pesticides, those made from natural resources. China recently set a goal of replanting 30 percent of its land in trees, with farm workers hired at regular wages to manage small plots of trees along city roads and railway stations. In 1989 the Inter-American Foundation, a U.S. government agency, gave $40,000 to farmers in Costa Rica who came up with the idea that they could save their land from erosion by planting trees on the bare hillsides of their country. In the small West African nation of Burkina Faso, since a drought began there in 1969, village women have had to walk more than 10 miles (16 kilometers) a day to gather wood for their cooking fires. And in 1985 government workers in the national capital, Ouagadougou, spent 20 percent of their salaries on firewood. But in 1989 a forestry professor at the national university, a graduate of Duke University in North Carolina, discovered a tree called *Gliricidia sepium,* which grows in Guatemala, Nicaragua, and other tropical countries and is considered the hardiest and fastest-growing tropical tree in the world. It is almost a weed, he says, impossible to kill; it withstands drought, has edible leaves, and has roots that fix nitrogen in the soil. The trees can be planted as living fences—marking property boundaries, fertilizing the fields of maize and sorghum that are Burkina Faso's main crop, and protecting the soil from wind and rain erosion after crops are harvested.

An important difference between biotechnology and sustainable agriculture is that the latter keeps humans in close contact with the earth. Biotechnology soars on the wings of science, while sustainable agriculture binds us to our natural environment. But neither science nor agriculture work in a vacuum. Any progress toward better food production and supply depends largely upon political and social factors—upon the actions of governments, the relations of nations, and the efforts of the various organizations that work to reduce hunger throughout the world. Sustainable agricultural methods used to be common in the United States, but in the past half-century our food production system has changed to one of high-energy use and technology. Unfortunately our high-technology system has been copied in many countries that do not have the money or the technical or managerial skills to manage it properly.

The last chapter of this book is concerned with these factors. More than any other global problem, the problem of hunger has many sides to it. It affects rich and poor nations alike. And within nations there are no longer any walls that protect the wealthy from the poor groups of people. Other global problems can be isolated or solved by direct measures. But hunger is complex and universal; it defies easy solutions.

A worker examines a one-year old gao plant in a millet field in eastern Niger. Gao trees planted in a millet field can triple or quadruple millet yield. Millet is a grain used for making flour in parts of Africa and Asia.

4

Food Production and Politics

As was said earlier, hunger is a complex problem. There are no easy solutions to providing the world's growing population with a dependable supply of adequate and nutritious food. Any such solutions must take into account the three major problems involved in the food production and delivery system.

These three problems are scientific, technological, and political. Chapter 1 dealt with hunger in its human aspects, how it affects people. In Chapter 2 we looked at the part that science plays in food production. Chapter 3 was concerned with technology's part in food production and supply. This last chapter pertains to the politics of food. The quality and quantity of food can be improved by scientific or technological methods, but merely increasing or improving food crops will not guarantee enough food for the world's population because food production and distribution are affected as much by politics as they are by science or technology.

Human society is made up of groups, with certain individuals elected or appointed to lead each group and to make decisions about matters affecting the group. The modern nation is made up of a number of groups living in a particular geographical area. In the past, these groups (or peoples) were different from each other in languages, customs, sets of religious beliefs, and so on. Some of these differences still exist. For example, Belgium has two different population groups, Flemish-speaking and French-speaking; Lebanon includes 24 different religious groups; and the Soviet Union's various "republics" contain an enormous variety of peoples with many different religions and cultures.

The history of most modern nations has often been one of conflicts among such groups, until one group came to rule the others. This group then established a government over the rest. The presence of a single government, a government *of* and *for* the people, is the most important feature of the modern nation. Governments of nations are not always accepted by their peoples; thus, today there are civil wars against the governments of such nations as Sudan, Afghanistan, and Nicaragua. But in most nations, governments make laws and set policies for their people on matters that affect national life.

Wars and famine often push people into refugee camps like this one in Somalia. Refugees depend on aid from organizations like the World Food Program of the United Nations.

One issue that is of great concern to governments is that of food production, distribution, and supply. Food production affects not only the relations of governments with their people but also their relations with other governments. The government of Sudan, which has been trying to put down a rebellion in its southern region since 1986, has often blocked delivery of food supplies to southern refugee camps and villages in order to starve the population into stopping support for the rebels. In Peru, which is the main supplier of cocaine to the United States and Europe, the government tries to cooperate with our government to stop the cocaine trade. But the Peruvian government is "on the spot" for a number of reasons. Coca leaves, the source of cocaine, are its largest export crop, with annual revenues of $540 million. The government badly needs this income for national development, and workers on the coca plantations can earn as much as $12 per day, about eight times the wages of workers on other Peruvian farms. Even if the government wanted to send troops into the coca-growing areas and force the growers to change to other crops, it would have difficulty in doing so because the growers are protected by a strong rebel organization, *Sendero Luminoso* (Shining Path), which controls the mountain regions where 75 percent of Peruvian coca is grown.

These examples show that political reasons often force governments to set food policies that cause problems for food production or supply. Many scientists believe that world hunger is basically political, and political methods must be used to deal with it. It is not enough merely to send shiploads of food from the rich countries to the poor ones. The rich countries need to help the poorer ones to increase their own food production, to grow better food crops so that they do not have to depend on food shipments to feed their people adequately.

Population Growth
The rapid growth of population in many countries has become a serious problem in terms of the food supply. In 1987 the UN Commis-

sion on the Environment warned that "the next few decades will be a greater danger to the world's food system than it may ever face again." The world's human population now stands at 5.3 billion, but if the present rate of growth continues it will reach 14.2 billion by A.D. 2120. Most of this growth is in the poorer countries, those least able to use science and technology to improve their food production system. Acting out of desperation, the poor in these countries are cutting down forests; planting crops in marginal land with poor soil or limited water resources; and allowing their livestock to overgraze pasturelands without replanting the grasses. They are destroying the environment that gives them their food—in short, just to be able to survive.

Obviously governments in these countries must either find ways to slow down population growth or to increase the food supply. They cannot do both. It is usually more difficult to control population growth than it is to improve the food supply because family customs, opposi-

A herd of skinny cattle graze on a field near N'Djamena, Chad. The problems of soil erosion and desert encroachment are made more serious by the hungry cattle.

tion from church or religious leaders, and economic problems in many countries help keep the birth rate at a high level. But even countries that have been able to gain support from their people for birth control programs often prefer to develop food crops for export rather than improve the food supply for their own people. Exports earn more money for the economy. Food crops do nothing for the economy; all they do is feed people!

One example of a government policy that favors export crops over food crops is found in Mexico. There the government encourages farmers who grow certain crops such as tomatoes or green vegetables to export rather than sell them to Mexican families. Most Mexican tomatoes end up in American markets. If they were sold in Mexican markets, they would add essential vitamins and nutrients to the Mexican diet, which is mostly based on corn and beans. But the growers can make up to twenty times as much per acre by shipping their tomatoes to the United States rather than selling them in Mexico. The government encourages them to export the crop because it brings badly needed dollars into Mexico to help the economy.

Sometimes policies intended to improve the food supply do the opposite. In Botswana, a small African country, the land is best suited for cattle grazing. The government decided to increase the number of cattle so that money from meat exports could be used to bring more land under cultivation for food crops. But the increase in cattle caused the pasturelands to become overgrazed. When the grass was all gone, desertification took place, and soon the land could not be used for food crops. By 1986 Botswana was having to import food. The country was spending more money for food imports than it received for its meat exports and was deeply in debt.

The choice of uses for land to grow food crops is often a matter of politics. Stephen Cobb, director of a United Nations project in the Niger River delta region in Africa, notes that the delta in its natural state is a wonderfully productive ecosystem; it supports a diverse wildlife, herders and their flocks of sheep and goats, fishers whose catch of tineni, a kind of sardine, is important to the diet of that region; and farmers. But government officials and planners think differently. When they look at the river they see huge dams that will change the river's course, provide water for irrigation of vast new farmlands, and help form rice paddies that will grow enough rice for the Niger Republic to export the crop, and thereby, earn money for the country to pay its foreign debts. The fact that this ecosystem has kept the population reasonably well-fed for centuries is not important to them.

Rich Nations, Poor Nations

The countries in the world today may be put into three groups, rich (or "developed"), not so rich but in fairly good shape financially, and poor ("less developed," or LDCs) as the UN describes them. One way to

Women pound corn for lunch at a primary school in Botswana. Note the open-air class in the background. The World Food Program provides assistance for supplementary food programs for primary school children, expectant and nursing mothers, and pre-school age children.

49

measure the difference among these groups is by their gross national product (GNP). GNP is the sum total of the goods and services produced in a country in one year. The income from GNP presents its wealth and is called per capita (or per person) income. There is a great difference between per capita income in the United States, which is around $16,000 a year, and those of Botswana or Ethiopia, which are around $100, the lowest in the world.

However, the difference in income does not mean that rich countries are absolutely rich and LDCs are absolutely poor. There are many people in the United States whose incomes are far below $16,000 and who must depend upon outside (usually government) help for their food. Likewise, many LDCs include in their populations families whose incomes and wealth are far above those of most American families. Also per capita income does not apply directly to people in the LDCs who grow enough food for their basic needs and need money only to buy the few things they cannot grow for themselves. The best that we can say about per capita income is that it is an average figure.

The Foreign Aid Program

An important part of the relationship between the rich nations and the poor nations is the foreign aid program. It is a government program— or group of programs—that sends aid from the United States and other industrial countries to poorer countries to help develop their economies. This aid includes military equipment, technical help by experts in various fields, and food aid. The wheat and corn grown on American farms in the Midwest is essential to the world's grain supply and has often been sent as aid to save people from starvation in such countries as Ethiopia and Bangladesh.

The most important foreign aid program in the United States is managed by a government agency, the U.S. Agency for International Development (USAID). This agency has had many other names since it was started after World War II. The original foreign aid program was called the Marshall Plan, named for General George C. Marshall, Chief of Staff of American forces in World War II and later Secretary of State. It was set up to help western Europe recover from the destruction of war. In recent years this aid has gone mostly to the poorer nations.

Some of these countries have used U.S. and other foreign aid and the technical help of experts with good results. The Republic of South Korea increased food production by 4.8 percent a year between 1963 and 1975 with foreign help, and by 1976 the country grew enough rice (the mainstay in the Korean diet) for its people. Foreign aid was partly responsible for the success of the Green Revolution in India and other Asian countries. American crop experts sent to Turkey have helped farmers in some regions of that country to harvest three crops a year!

One problem with foreign aid is that it is given at times for political reasons. Total U.S. aid to the LDCs during the period 1980–85 was $34 billion. However, 50 percent of this amount went to ten countries and nearly one-third ($10.65 billion) to just two, Egypt and Israel. These countries were favored because they were—and are—important to American foreign policy either as allies or as supporters or protectors of U.S. interests in troubled areas of the world.

In the last ten years or so, foreign aid to the LDCs has come more from international groups or organizations than directly from individual countries. The UN has a large number of food-aid projects itself, as do UN agencies such as the Food and Agriculture Organization (FAO) and UNICEF. The World Bank (International Bank for Reconstruction and Development), a banking organization of many governments, has probably the largest number of aid programs. It is the closest thing we have to a bank that serves the whole world.

The Problem of Debt
In recent years the debts that poor nations owe to rich nations for

foreign aid have become a serious problem, affecting not only the food supply but also the economies of these nations and their very survival. To explain this problem, we should know that there are two kinds of foreign aid, grants and loans. Grants are like gifts at Christmas or birthdays; they do not have to be repaid. In times of starvation in countries such as India, the United States sends supplies of grain and

A World Bank loan was used to construct a huge irrigation system in the Sudan. These women are collecting drinking water at a recently built supply point.

other food crops to help people without expecting—or wanting—to be paid back.

Aid in the form of loans is another matter. The lending agency—whether it is USAID, the UN, the World Bank, or private banks—sets an interest rate and a date for repayment of the loan, just as a bank does with a home mortgage. The interest rate is usually very low, 2 or 3 percent, but it is due once every year.

In the 1960s and 1970s many of the poor nations borrowed large amounts of money from these agencies to finance their economic development. They borrowed money for dams, highways, railroads, development of new industries, sewer and drinking-water projects for their cities, farm equipment, and other needs. They also borrowed billions of dollars, rubles, pounds, or yen for weapons for their new armies and air forces.

Some of the poorer nations who had important oil resources, such as Mexico, Nigeria, and Algeria, borrowed this money with the expectation that oil revenues would pay for their loans. Other poor nations that do not have oil, such as Turkey and Brazil, were forced to pay high prices for the oil they needed for their industrial development. None of this seemed to matter as long as there was plenty of money around and the world price of oil was high. But in the 1980s the bottom fell out of the oil market. Suddenly the oil-producing countries began receiving less and less money for their oil. World prices of export crops, such as coffee, and of phosphates also went down; and as interest payments came due, governments could not pay them. In order to meet their debts, these governments borrowed more money at higher interest rates to pay the interest on the original loans, putting themselves deeper and deeper in debt.

The African country of Sudan is a good example of the debt problem. In the 1970s experts had predicted that the country would become the "breadbasket" of East Africa and the Middle East, growing enough food to feed its own people and those of an entire region. There was even some oil, discovered by the U.S. Exxon Company in the southwestern part of the country. But for many reasons Sudan has become a basket case rather than a breadbasket. By 1989 the government owed more than $12 billion to the World Bank and other creditors and did not have even enough money coming in to pay the interest on this amount.

The debt problem is only one of many factors affecting food production, but it is an important one. If a country has to spend all its revenues to pay interest on its debts, there will be nothing left over to pay for improvements in the food supply. One solution to the problem has been developed by the World Bank. The bank now sets strict rules that a borrowing country must follow before it can receive any new loans or defer interest on old loans. Ghana, in West Africa, agreed to follow the new rules in 1983. The government eliminated thousands of jobs, lowered the value of its money, and cut prices on basic foods such as bread and cooking oil. As of today, Ghana is out of debt and eligible for new loans.

One foreign aid program for the poor nations is based entirely on peoples' concern for human needs. In recent years churches, private foundations, and business firms have been making loans to groups of people mainly to help them improve food production and become self-sufficient. In Bolivia, for example, a U.S. foundation gives $50 in cash to groups of village women to buy vegetables directly from farmers and resell them in the open-air markets of the Bolivian capital, La Paz. Because they had no cash, the women had to buy the vegetables on credit, paying 10 percent interest and often receiving spoiled crops. These small-scale projects will not solve the huge problems involved in increasing the food supply in most of the world, but they could provide an incentive to the "poorest of the poor" in many countries, giving them a chance to improve their lives.

The United States in a Hungry World

As we saw in the first chapter, Americans until recently have thought of hunger as something that affects people in other parts of the world but not in their own country. Yet today, hunger is not only widespread, but is also affecting other social groups besides the poor. Silicon Valley, an area of high-technology industries and research firms that formerly paid high salaries, now serves 35,000 people a month from its food bank; most of them are ex-employees of these companies, laid off from their jobs. The number of families applying for food stamps in the steel-making cities of Ohio in 1988 was 70 percent more than in 1982. Florida, now the nation's fourth largest state in population, has attracted large numbers of wealthy retired people, but its population also includes many poor families—migrant workers, Hispanics, and refugees from Haiti and other Caribbean countries. It is estimated that one out of four Florida residents lives at or below poverty levels.

Conclusions

Solving the problem of world hunger will require not only improving food crops, increasing production, and lowering food costs. It will also require a system of distribution to bring adequate and nutritious food to every man, woman, and child on this earth.

Yet, it is still far easier for scientists and specialists in biotechnology, agriculture, and other fields to work together— regardless of their countries of origin—to improve the world food supply, than it is for the governments of their countries to cooperate in working to end world hunger. In the past, groups used the resources around them wisely to benefit all persons in the group; they were good stewards of the land and did not exploit it. Perhaps the best example of good stewardship is that of the Native American tribes; even today tribes such as the Hopis in New Mexico do not exploit their land, but use it for the benefit of the whole group. But greed and ignorance, along with rapid population growth, threaten our food supply as never before in history. Our resources of land, water, and air are being used up faster than they can be replaced.

Is there any hope that we humans can solve not only the hunger problem but also other and equally difficult world problems? One answer to this question lies with the United Nations. Countries may be able to produce enough food to feed the majority of their people as the United States does, but often their success comes at the expense of other, poorer countries. Only the UN, since its membership includes all nations, large and small, rich and poor, can deal on a global basis with global problems.

Thus, it is encouraging that the month of September 1990 marked the first attempt by all the nations of the world to deal with the hunger problem through the UN. Candlelight vigils, beginning in New Zealand and sweeping across the time zones of the globe, called world attention to the first-ever Summit Conference of national leaders at the UN on September 29–30. It was a political conference, reminding us that politics is an essential part of the problem of world hunger. The candles people lighted in their cities and towns carried a simple message—"light a candle for the future of children everywhere." For without healthy children there cannot be healthy adults. This is what the peoples of the world are really saying to their governments, and governments owe nothing less to their peoples. The leaders' decision at the Conference to try to end child malnutrition on today's scale by the year 2000 is a step in that direction, a promise to be kept.

Glossary

agriculture—The cultivation of plants and use of land to grow food crops.

aquaculture—The growing of food crops, including fish, in water.

aquifer—A source of water found underground in layers of rock.

biotechnology—Changing plant and animal genetic structure by scientific methods; also *genetic engineering* (a combination of biology and engineering).

carbohydrates—An important class of food substances, including sugars, starches, etc.

deforestation—Removal or loss of forests by human actions, such as cutting or burning.

desertification—The spread of deserts over cultivated areas, by human or natural action.

ecosystem—The sum total of living and non-living elements in a particular environment.

environment—The particular conditions that surround a community, either social or biological.

erosion—The wearing away or removal of soil from an environment, usually by weather but frequently due to human action.

evolution—The process of change in organisms or societies.

exports—Products sold or exchanged by a country outside its borders to bring in income or needed materials.

greenhouse effect—Buildup of CO_2 (carbon dioxide) and other gases in the atmosphere to cause a warming of temperatures and perhaps other climatic changes.

GNP/GDP—Gross National Product/Gross Domestic Product, the sum total of goods and services produced by a country as a measurement of national income.

hybrid—A plant or animal that is the result of the combination of the genetic characteristics of two types or species.

imports—The goods or services bought or received by exchange from one country to another.

irrigation—The use of water from sources below the earth's surface to grow crops, as opposed to natural rainfall.

malnutrition—Lack of the nutrients, vitamins and minerals necessary for a balanced healthy diet.

nutrition—The process by which plants and animals take in, digest, and absorb food.

ozone layer (ozonosphere)—A layer of the earth's atmosphere, 20-30 miles (32-48 km) up, which absorbs and filters the ultraviolet rays of the sun in order to make life possible on the planet.

photosynthesis—The formation of carbohydrates in living plants.

protein—A very large class of substances, often called amino acids, which are essential to the growth of cells in living plants and animals.

technology—The scientific application of knowledge for practical purposes.

Further Reading

Books

Berg, Allan. *Malnutrition: What Can Be Done?* Baltimore, Md.: Johns Hopkins Press, 1987.

Byron, William. *The Causes of World Hunger*. New York: Paulist Press, 1982.

Crosson, Pierre, ed. *The Cropland Crisis: Myth or Reality?* Baltimore, Md.: Johns Hopkins Press, 1982.

Doyle, Jack. *Altered Harvest: Agriculture, Genetics, and the Fate of the World's Food Supply*. New York: Viking Press, 1985.

Glaeser, Bernhard. *The Green Revolution Revisited*. London: George Allen & Unwin, 1987.

Juma, Calestous. *The Gene Hunters: Biotechnology and the Scramble for Seeds*. Princeton, N.J.: Princeton University Press, 1989.

Kloppenburg, Jack. *First the Seed: The Political Economy of Plant Biotechnology, 1492-2000*. New York: Cambridge University Press, 1989.

————, ed. *Seeds and Sovereignty*. Durham, N.C.: Duke University Press, 1988.

Lappe, Frances and Joseph Collins. *Food First*, revised edition. New York: Ballantine Books, 1978.

———— and C. Dean Freudenberger. *Food, Farming and Justice*. The Lutheran Church, U.S.A., 1985.

Molnar, Joseph and Henry Kinnucan, eds. *Biotechnology and the New Agricultural Revolution*. Boulder, Colo.: Westview Press, 1989.

Myers, Norman, ed. *GAIA: An Atlas of Planet Management*. Garden City, N.Y.: Doubleday, 1984.

Shore, William, ed. *Louder the Words*. New York: Random House, 1989.

Periodicals

African Farmer. San Francisco, Calif.: The Hunger Project. Articles on African agriculture.

ARAMCO WORLD. Houston, Tex.: Aramco Services, formerly the Arabian-American Oil Company. Articles on agriculture and technology in the Middle East.

Hunger Notes. Washington, D.C.: World Education Hunger Service. Both general-interest and technical articles on world hunger issues.

New Internationalists. P.O. Box 255, Lewiston, N.Y. 14092.

Nutrition Action. Washington, D.C.: Center for Science in the Public Interest. Newsletter.

The Other Side. 300 West Apsley Street, Philadephia, Penn.. 19144.

SEEDS. 222 East Lake Drive, Decatur, Ga. 30030. A church publication.

Sojourners. P.O. Box 29272, Washington, D.C. 20017.

For Further Information

American Friends Service Committee
1501 Cherry Street
Philadelphia, PA 19102

Bread for the World
802 Rhode Island Avenue N.E.
Washington, DC 20018

Center for Science in the Public Interest (CSPI)
1501 16th Street N.W.
Washington, DC 20036

Church World Service/CROP
P.O. Box 968
Elkhart, IN 46515

Conservation International
1015 18th Street N.W.
Washington, DC 20036

ECHO (Educational Concerns for Hunger Organization)
17430 Durrance Rd.
North Fort Myers, FL 33917

Food and Agriculture Organization of the United Nations
Liaison Office for North America
1001 22 Street N.W.
Suite 300
Washington, DC 20437

Friends of the Third World
611 West Wayne Street
Fort Wayne, IN 46802

The Hunger Project
1388 Sutter Street
San Francisco, CA 94109-5452

IMPACT
110 Maryland Avenue N.E.
Washington, DC 20002

Institute for Food and Development Policy (Food First)
1885 Mission Street
San Francisco, CA 94103-3584

National Audubon Society
950 Third Avenue
New York, NY 10022

Overseas Development Council
1717 Massachusetts Ave., N.W.
Washington, DC 20036

Oxfam America
115 Broadway
Boston, MA 02116

Presbyterian Hunger Program
Presbyterian Church (U.S.A.)
475 Riverside Drive
Room 1268
New York, NY 10115

RESULTS
236 Massachusetts Ave., N.E.
Suite 110
Washington, DC 20002

Science for the People
897 Main Street
Cambridge, MA 02139

World Hunger Education Service
1317 G Street N.W.
Washington, DC 20005

Worldwatch Institute
1776 Massachusetts Ave., N.W.
Washington, DC 20036

Index

A Abyei, Sudan, 5-6
Afghanistan, 45
Africa, 6, 23, 30, 33, 40, *43*, 48
agriculture, 15, 19, 28, 30, 55
Alar, 35
algae, 40
amaranth, 29
Amazon River, 20
Andes Mountains, 20, 37
aquaculture, 40-41
Aral Sea, 24

B Barash, David, 27
Bass, Thomas, 10-11
biogas, 40
biotechnology, 30, 35-36, 38, 41-42, 55
"blue corn," 29
Borlaug, Norman, 30, 36
Botswana, 48-50
Brazil, 17, 22, 29, 53
Brown, Lester, 13, 24-25, 35
Burkina Faso, 42

C China, 19, 40-42
chlorophyll, 38
climate
changes in, 25
effect on food, 15
Cobb, Stephen, 48
coca, as source of cocaine, 46
"Corn Belt," U.S., 19

cotton, in USSR, 24
crop rotation, 41
Cusack, David, 32

D deforestation, 21-23
desertification, 23, 48

E East Africa, 53
ecosystem, Niger Delta, 48-49
Egypt, 17, 27, 51
erosion, 22, 42, 47
Ethiopia, 6, 9, 50
evolution, 26-29
technological, 28-29

F famine, 25
fermentation, 35
fish farming, 41
Florida, 34, 42, 55
food crops, exportable, 22
and world hunger, 55
food production, 13-16
and deserts, 23
and human skills, 19
and overgrazing, 48
and technology, 29, 34
and tropical rain forests, 22
and water resources, 24
foreign aid program, U.S., 50, 52-54
Frostban, 38

G gene banks, 37

"gene-tailored crops," 38
genetic engineering, 21, 36-38
Gliricidia sepium, 42
Gore, Sen. Albert, Jr., 22
Green Revolution, 30, 32, 35, 51
"greenhouse effect," 15, 25
Guatemala, 9, 42

H Haiti, 22, 29, 55
Harris, Myles, 6, 12
Hastings, Florida, 34
Howard, Robert, 17

I Incas, 20-21
system of agriculture, 20
India, 10, 50
irrigation
systems of, 18-19
overuse of, 23

J de Jesus, Maria, 6, 12

K Kansas, wheat crop in, 16, 30
kaolin clay, 17
Kleckner, Dean, 34
kwashiorkor, 11-12

L Langer, Susanna, 29
Latin America, 33, 39
legumes, 37, 41
low technology, systems of, 39-40

M Madagascar, 17, 22
malnutrition, 9, 25, 30
marasmus, 11

Mayas, civilization of, 17
McKibben, Bill, 21, 27
Mexico
    and food crops, 48
    oil resources, 53
Middle East, 15, 30, 53
millet, 39, 43
N Nepal, 17, 29
Nicaragua, 45
Niger, 42, 49
nitrogen-fixing plants, 37-38, 42
O organic farming, 30
    and fertilizers, 41
ozone layer, 25
P Pakistan, 19, 28
Peru, 16, 46
population growth, 34-35, 46, 47
    threat to food supply, 55
protein, 20, 39,-40

S Sahara desert, 15, 23
Sahel, 15
science of food production, 21
Sendero Luminoso, 46
soils and soil fertility, 16
sorghum, 39
soybeans, 39
Sudan, 5, 9, 45-46, 52-53
    as breadbasket of region, 54
T technology of food, 12, 15, 26
Turkey, 15, 50-51, 53
U UNICEF, 11-12
UN Commission on the Environment, 46-47
United Nations, 23, 34, 45, 49, 53, 56
United States, 33-35, 46, 48, 50, 55

USAID, 50, 53
V Vietnam, 6
W Washington, D.C., 24
weather, as distinct from climate, 15
wheat, hybrid, 30
winged bean, 39
World Bank (International Bank for Reconstruction and Development), 51-54
World Commission on the Environment and Development, 34
World Food Program, 45, 49
World War II, 51
Worldwatch Institute, 24, 25

About the Author

Dr. William Spencer is the author of several books for young people, and was for thirty-five years the annual Middle Eastern articles contributor to *The World Book Year Book*. Dr. Spencer is on the board of directors of ACORN (Alachua County Organization for Rural Needs), a rural health clinic that brings medical services to low-income families, and is also involved with the Central Florida Community Action Agency, a group that distributes surplus goods, such as flour and butter, to the needy. His wife Elizabeth Bouvier Spencer is an artist.